This edition published by Parragon Books Ltd in 2015 and distributed by

Parragon Inc.
440 Park Avenue South, 13th Floor
New York, NY 10016
www.parragon.com

Written and retold by Etta Saunders, Annie Baker, Steve Smallman,
Ronne Randall, Anne Marie Ryan
Illustrated by Simon Mendez, Barroux, Dubravka Kolanovic, Mei Matsuoka,
Tamsin and Natalie Hinrichsen, Erica-Jane Waters, Gavin Scott, Gail Yerrill,
Jacqueline East, Karen Sapp, Steve Whitlow
Edited by Rebecca Wilson
Cover illustrated by Deborah Allwright

Every effort has been made to acknowledge the contributors to this book.
If we have made any errors, we will be pleased to rectify them in future editions.

ISBN 978-1-4723-5464-8

Printed in China

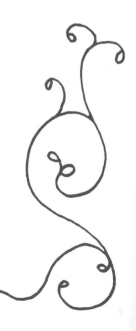

A Collection of
Stories for
2
Year Olds

PaRragon

Bath • New York • Cologne • Melbourne • Delhi
Hong Kong • Shenzhen • Singapore • Amsterdam

Contents

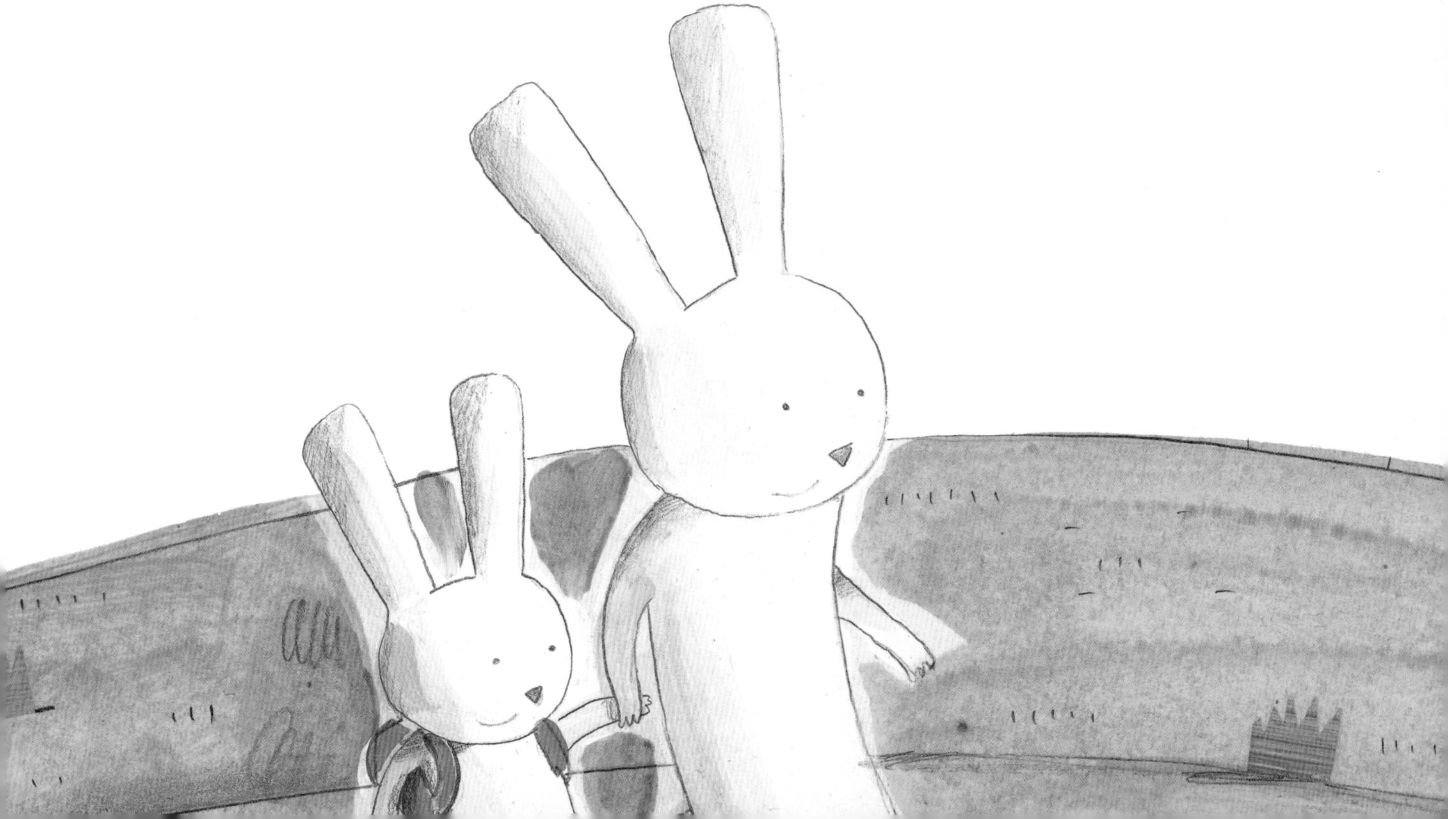

Goldilocks and the Three Bears

Once upon a time, a little girl named Goldilocks
was playing in the woods near her home.
A yummy smell drifted down the pebbly path.

Goldilocks followed
the smell to a little house.
She knocked on the front door.

KNOCK, KNOCK!

But there was no one home.

Goldilocks was so hungry, she followed the smell inside.

In the kitchen, she saw a big bowl, a medium-sized bowl, and a teeny-tiny bowl of porridge.

First, Goldilocks tried the porridge in the biggest bowl. But it was too cold!

Next, she tried the porridge in the medium-sized bowl. But it was too hot!

Finally, she tried the porridge in the smallest bowl. It was just right, and she ate it all up.

Then Goldilocks went into
the living room for a rest.

Goldilocks sat in the big chair.
But it was too high up!

She sat in the
medium-sized chair.
But it was too squishy!

Then Goldilocks sat in the tiny chair, and it was just right! But then ...

CR-R-R-RACK!

The chair broke into teeny-tiny pieces!
"Oh!" Goldilocks gasped in surprise.
"Perhaps I should lie down instead."

Upstairs, Goldilocks lay down on the big bed. But it was too hard!

Then she lay down on the medium-sized bed. But it was too soft!

Finally, she lay down on the teeny-tiny bed. It was just right. And she fell fast asleep.

ZZZZZZZZZzzzzzzz

Meanwhile, a big daddy bear, a medium-sized mommy bear, and a teeny-tiny baby bear returned home.

They had been for a walk while their hot porridge cooled down.

"Someone's been eating my porridge," roared Daddy Bear.

"Someone's been eating my porridge, too," growled Mommy Bear.

"Look!" squeaked Baby Bear. "My porridge is all gone!"

The three bears went into the living room.

"Someone's been sitting in my chair!" roared Daddy Bear.

"Someone's been sitting in my chair, too," growled Mommy Bear.

"Someone's been sitting in my chair," squeaked Baby Bear, "and they've broken it!"

The three bears went upstairs.

"Someone's been sleeping in my bed!" roared Daddy Bear.

"Someone's been sleeping in my bed, too," growled Mommy Bear.

"Someone's been sleeping in my bed," squeaked Baby Bear, "and she's still there!"

At that moment, Goldilocks woke up. When she saw the three bears, she ran out of their house and all the way home!

She never visited the house of the three bears ever again.

Muddypaws' New Friends

Ben and his puppy, Muddypaws, were best
friends. They did everything together.

But when Ben went to school, Muddypaws had to stay at home with nobody to play with.

Then, one day, Ben said, "Come on, Muddypaws,
let's go to school!"

Muddypaws was very excited ...

and pulled on

his leash all the way!

But they didn't go to Ben's school. They went to …

Puppy School!

Two other puppies came over to say hello. Droopy, a little puppy with big, dangly ears, was a little bit shy. But his friend Patch wasn't!

"Muddypaws, why don't you play with your new friends till it's time to start school?" said Ben. The three puppies chased each other around and around the yard.

The three puppies found a big puddle.

Splish!

Droopy tiptoed in up to the bottom of his ears.

Splash!

Muddypaws jumped in up to his tummy.

Splosh!

Patch jumped in up to his collar!

Then it was time to start the class. The first lesson was "Sitting."

"SIT!"

Droopy sat.

Muddypaws rolled over!

Patch shook water all over the place!

The second lesson was "Fetching." Everyone had brought a rolled-up sock for their puppies to fetch.

"Fetch!"

Droopy picked up his sock.

Muddypaws picked up his sock, too!

Patch pounced on his. Then he shook it until it unrolled, flew up in the air, and ...

... landed on Muddypaws' head!
Muddypaws and Droopy happily trotted back together.
"Good boy!" laughed Ben. "You fetched your sock!"

Before the end of the class,
the teacher wanted to try the
"Sitting" lesson again.

"SIT!"

Droopy sat.

Muddypaws woofed
happily. But he didn't sit.

Patch chased his tail.
He didn't like to sit still!

Ben thought he'd try
one last time ...

When it was time to go home, Muddypaws was a little bit sad to say goodbye to Droopy and Patch.

"Don't worry, Muddypaws!" said Ben. "You'll see them again next week!"

So with a happy goodbye "woof," Muddypaws headed
back home with Ben, his very best friend of all!

The Three Little Pigs

Once upon a time, there were three little pigs. One day Mommy Pig told them,

"You must build your own houses. But watch out for the big bad wolf!"

The first little pig bought some straw from a farmer to build his house.

"This straw will not make a strong house," the farmer warned him. But the little pig did not listen.

The big bad wolf saw the little pig's straw house.
"Little pig, little pig, let me in," he growled.
"Not by the hairs on my chinny-chin-chin!"
the little pig shouted back.

"Well, I'll huff and I'll puff,
and I'll blow your house down!"

said the wolf. And he did.
   So the poor little pig ran away.

43

The second little pig bought some sticks from a woodcutter for his house.

"These sticks will not make a strong house," the woodcutter warned him. But the second little pig did not listen.

The big bad wolf saw the little pig's stick house.

"Little pig, little pig, let me in," he growled.

"Not by the hairs on my chinny-chin-chin!" the little pig shouted back.

"Well, I'll huff and I'll puff,
and I'll blow your house down!"

said the wolf. And he did.
So the poor little pig ran away.

The third little pig bought some bricks from a builder for his house.

"These bricks will make a good, strong house," the builder told him. The third little pig was very pleased.

Just as the house was finished and the third little pig had started making his dinner, his two brothers came running up the path.

"Let us in!" they shouted. "The wolf is coming!"

So he did.

The big bad wolf saw the little pig's brick house.

"Little pig, little pig,
let me in,"

he roared.

"Not by the hairs on my chinny-chin-chin!" the third little pig shouted.

"Well, I'll huff and I'll puff,
and I'll blow your house down!"

said the wolf ... but the brick house stood firm.

49

The wolf looked for another way in. He climbed up to the roof of the house and slid down the chimney—straight into a pot of boiling-hot soup.

The wolf ran howling into the night, never to be seen again, and the three little pigs lived happily ever after, all together in the strong brick house.

I Love You When

I love you when it's warm and sunny.

I love you when you're being funny.

I love you when it's wet outside.

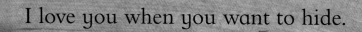

I love you when you want to hide.

I love you when
you giggle ...

when you wiggle ...

when you wriggle ...

I love you when you're snuggly.

I love you when you're huggly.

I love you when you say, "I love you, too."

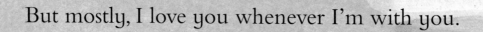

But mostly, I love you whenever I'm with you.

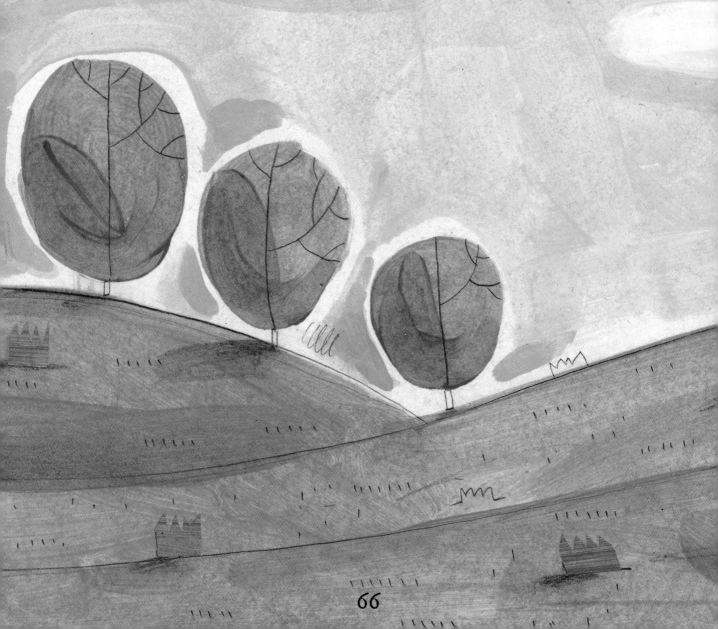

Humpty Dumpty

Humpty Dumpty sat on a wall,
Humpty Dumpty had a great fall.
All the king's horses and all the king's men
Couldn't put Humpty together again!

Ring Around the Rosie

Ring around the rosie,
A pocket full of posies.

Ashes! Ashes!
We all fall down.

Little Bo-Peep

Little Bo-Peep has lost her sheep
And doesn't know where to find them.

72

Leave them alone,
And they'll come home,
Wagging their tails behind them.

The Grand Old Duke of York

The grand old Duke of York,
He had ten thousand men.
He marched them up to the top of the hill,
And he marched them down again.

When they were up, they were up.
And when they were down, they were down.
And when they were only halfway up,
They were neither up nor down.

Hey Diddle Diddle

Hey diddle diddle, the
cat and the fiddle,

The cow jumped over the moon.

The little dog laughed to see such fun,
And the dish ran away with the spoon!

The Wheels On the Bus

The wheels on the bus go
round and round!
Round and round!
Round and round!

The wheels on the bus go
round and round.
All day long.

Baa, Baa, Black Sheep

Baa, baa, black sheep,
Have you any wool?

Yes sir, yes sir,
Three bags full.

One for the master ...

And one for the dame ...

And one for the little boy
Who lives down the lane.

Little Miss Muffet

Little Miss Muffet
Sat on a tuffet,
Eating her curds and whey.

Along came a spider,
Who sat down beside her,

And frightened Miss Muffet away!

Row, Row, Row Your Boat

(Mime a rowing action throughout.)

Row, row, row your boat,
Gently down the stream.

Merrily, merrily,
merrily, merrily,

Life is but a dream.

Mary Had a Little Lamb

Mary had a little lamb,
Its fleece was white as snow,
And everywhere that Mary went
The lamb was sure to go.

It followed her to school one day,
Which was against the rule.
It made the children laugh and play
To see a lamb at school.

The Itsy Bitsy Spider

The itsy bitsy spider
Climbed up the water spout.
Down came the rain
And washed the spider out.

Out came the sun

And dried up all the rain.
And the itsy bitsy spider
Climbed up the spout again.

This Little Piggy

(Pretend each of the child's toes is a little piggy.
Begin with the biggest toe, and finish by tickling under the child's foot.)

This little piggy
went to market,

This little piggy
stayed at home,

This little piggy
had roast beef,

This little piggy
had none,

And this little piggy cried,
"Wee, wee, wee!"
all the way home.

Twinkle, Twinkle, Little Star

Twinkle, twinkle, little star,
How I wonder what you are!
Up above the world so high,
Like a diamond in the sky.

When the blazing sun is gone,
When he nothing shines upon,
Then you show your little light,
Twinkle, twinkle, all the night.

Then the traveler in the dark,
Thanks you for your tiny spark,
He could not see which way to go,
If you did not twinkle so.

In the dark blue sky you keep,
And often through my curtains peep,
For you never shut your eye,
Till the sun is in the sky.

As your bright and tiny spark,
Lights the traveler in the dark.
Though I know not what you are,

Twinkle, twinkle, little star.